W9-AWT-197

GREAT
SCIENTIFIC
THEORIES

Gravity

Nick Hunter

capstone

Published by Raintree, a Capstone Imprint
1710 Roe Crest Drive, North Mankato, Minnesota 56003.
www.mycapstone.com

Library of Congress Cataloging-in-Publication Data
Library of Congress Cataloging-in-Publication data is available on the Library of Congress website.

ISBN 978-1-4109-8729-7 (library hardcover) — 978-1-4109-8734-1 (paperback) — 978-1-4109-8738-9 (eBook PDF)

Summary:
This book looks at the historical controversies that surround the theory of gravity and tells the stories of the scientists who worked on the theory. It also examines how they arrived at the theory of gravity, how it was tested, and what impact the theory has had on our understanding of science today.

This book has been officially leveled by using the F&P Text Level Gradient™ System.

Editorial Credits
Helen Cox Cannons, editor; Terri Poburka, designer; Morgan Walters, media researchers; Steve Walker, production specialist

We would like to thank Dr. Rohini Giles at NASA's Jet Propulsion Laboratory for her invaluable help in the preparation of this book.

Photo Credits
We would like to thank the following for permission to reproduce photographs: Alamy Stock Photo: ClassicStock, (paper texture) design element throughout, Ian Dagnall, (lines) design element throughout; Getty Images: Bettmann, (lines) design element throughout, Daniel Berehulak, (writing background) design element, UniversalImagesGroup, Cover; iStockphoto: duncan1890, 4, gremlin, 5; Newscom: MARK GARLICK/SCIENCE PHOTO LIBRARY, 6, N.A.S.A/SIPA, 7, 8, Oxford Science Archive Heritage Images, 9, 10, Pictures From History, 11, 12; North Wind Picture Archives, 13; Shutterstock: alexaldo, 14, archideaphoto, 15, Arevik, 16, Everett Historical, 17, Fedor Selivanov, 18, fixer00, 19, 20, fstockfoto, 21, Golden Shrimp, 22, martinho Smart, 23, 24, Monkey Business Images, 25, Mopic, 26, Nikolayenko Yekaterina, 28, Vadim Sadovski, top right 28, middle left 28, Yurkoman, bottom right 28.

Printed and bound in the USA
010365F17

TABLE OF CONTENTS

Testing Theories. 4

What is Gravity?. 6

On the Road to Gravity. 8

Newton's Law of Gravity 12

Reactions and Rifts. 16

Einstein Explains 20

Why Does Gravity Matter?. 26

Quiz 28

Timeline 29

Glossary 30

Read More 31

Index 32

Some words are shown in bold, **like this**.
You can find out what they mean by
looking in the glossary.

TESTING THEORIES

Science is all about trying to explain the world around us. Scientists try to explain how everything works, from the tiniest particle of matter to the gigantic stars and planets that make up the universe. A **theory** is used to try to answer some of the biggest questions about life, the universe, and everything.

New Ideas

For hundreds of years, scientists have tried to explain the world and beyond by coming up with ideas about the way things work. A scientific idea is known as a **hypothesis**. When scientists believe they have collected enough **evidence** that shows their idea is correct, the idea becomes a theory.

Giant telescopes like this one are used to observe deep space to find evidence to support scientific theories.

Scientists carry out experiments to test their ideas.

Theories

Scientists test new theories all the time, but their ideas are built on the theories of scientists who came before them. Some of history's greatest scientists completely changed the way people thought about the world.

How Ideas Change

Before the ideas of modern science began to develop in the 1500s, people had many ideas that we now know to be untrue. Alchemists believed that other metals could be changed into gold. They searched for the secrets of **alchemy**. Later, scientists were able to prove that one metal cannot be turned into another.

The Theory of Gravity

The theory of **gravity** is one of the most important steps in the history of science. It came from the brilliant mind of Isaac Newton. But the story of the theory of gravity would not be complete without the contribution of many different scientists.

WHAT IS GRAVITY?

Why does the rain fall? Why do rivers flow to the sea? Why does everything that goes up come back down again? The answer to all of these questions, and many more, is gravity.

Invisible Force

Gravity is an invisible **force**. We can't see, hear ,or taste it, but we can see its effects. Try dropping a book and you'll see gravity in action when it falls to the ground. As well as all the objects that we own, the force of gravity holds each and every one of us on the surface of planet Earth.

Gravity means that everything on Earth is attracted towards the center of our planet, so water flows downhill.

Universal Force

Gravity does not just affect us and the things around us. It is the force that keeps Earth **orbiting**, or moving around, the sun and holds the universe together. The force of gravity attracts all objects toward each other. However, we only really notice the gravitational force of truly massive objects like planets.

PLAYING GOLF ON THE MOON

The moon is smaller than Earth, so the force of gravity is about one-sixth as strong as it is on Earth. In 1971, American astronaut Alan Shepard decided to carry out his own experiment by playing golf on the moon. The moon's weaker gravity meant that Shepard's golf shots went "miles and miles and miles." That's because the gravity on the moon wasn't strong enough to hold the ball down.

ON THE ROAD TO GRAVITY

Given how important gravity is, it's amazing that for thousands of years, no one really had a good explanation of what it was and why it happened. This was partly because ancient peoples' ideas about how the universe worked were based on one big error — they thought Earth was the center of the universe.

Ancient Greeks

Ancient Greek thinkers like Aristotle (384–322 BC) believed that the sun, planets, and other stars all orbited around Earth. It seemed natural to them that everything should be pulled toward

Arabic scholars introduced more math and measurements to the study of science.

Earth's center. Greek thinkers also believed that everything was made from four things they called elements. Earth and water fell to the ground, while fire and air tried to escape.

Arabs and Indians

In later centuries, Arab and Indian thinkers were the first to suggest that there might be some kind of attraction between Earth and other objects. However, it was not until the 1500s that scientists began to get a clearer picture of the universe.

Sun at the Center

In May 1543, Nicolaus Copernicus (1473–1543) published his theory that the sun was actually at the center of our **solar system**, orbited by Earth and other planets. This was an amazing idea. It led to many advances in science. Johannes Kepler built on Copernicus' ideas by plotting the paths of the planets around the sun.

BIOGRAPHY

JOHANNES KEPLER

Johannes Kepler (1571–1630) was a German astronomer and mathematician. He was interested in **astronomy** from an early age. The theory of gravity would not have been possible without Kepler's theories about the movement of planets.

Galileo and Motion of Objects

Galileo Galilei (1564–1642) was born in Pisa, Italy. He was a brilliant scientist and inventor. Galileo designed his own telescope and used it to discover four moons orbiting the planet Jupiter. This convinced him that Copernicus was right, and Earth was not the center of the universe.

In Trouble

When Galileo's ideas were printed, he found himself in trouble with the **Roman Catholic Church**. The powerful church taught its followers that everything orbited around Earth. They ordered the scientist to be imprisoned in his house.

Galileo was a great scientist who had a talent for getting himself into trouble.

Gravity

Galileo could still work and he continued to investigate gravity. He found that a **pendulum** would swing at the same rate no matter what object was on the end of it. He decided that all objects must fall at the same rate, no matter how heavy they are. Galileo's experiments also told him that objects falling or rolling down a slope would accelerate, or get faster, because of this mysterious force. These discoveries helped to start a revolution in science.

LEANING TOWER OR TALL TALE?

After Galileo died, a legend grew that he had tested how fast different objects would fall by dropping them from the famous leaning tower of Pisa in Italy. This may not be a true story. However, Galileo did prove that in a **vacuum**, a totally empty space with no air resistance, heavy and light objects would fall to the ground at the same speed. This is due to gravity.

NEWTON'S LAW OF GRAVITY

Galileo's experiments solved many questions about how objects moved, but he did not try to explain why this happened. That was left to Isaac Newton (1643–1727).

A Brilliant Mind

Isaac Newton's father died before Isaac was born. Having no father meant that Isaac had a difficult childhood. But it was clear that he was brilliant at math and science. At Cambridge University, Newton tried to unravel some of the biggest math problems of the day. This would help him in solving the mystery of gravity. But in 1665, Cambridge University was closed because of an outbreak of a disease called plague. Stuck in his childhood home in Lincolnshire, England, Newton worked secretly on the ideas that would make his name.

Newton's ideas also advanced knowledge of mathematics, light, and many areas of science.

Theory of Universal Gravitation

Newton did not publish his Theory of Universal Gravitation, as it was called, until 1687, more than 20 years after he claimed to have thought of it. He first mentioned it when discussing the movement of **comets** with his friend and fellow scientist Edmond Halley (1656–1742). Maybe Newton thought it was not that important, but the theory caused a sensation.

NEWTON AND THE APPLE

You may have heard that an apple falling from a tree inspired Newton's theory, but did it really happen? The story was written after Newton's death by someone who said he had heard it from Newton himself. But Newton never told the story in his own writings.

What Did Newton's Theory Say?

Newton's Theory of Universal Gravitation was able to explain both the movements of vast objects in space and what happens when an apple falls from a tree. Other scientists had been able to suggest some parts of the theory, but Newton was able to support everything with math. Almost everything in his theory is still used by scientists today.

Universal and Attractive

According to Newton, gravity is universal, meaning that it behaves in the same way anywhere in the universe, on any object. Gravity is also an attractive force between all objects, pulling them together. It acts on objects over a distance, such as between Earth and the moon. Newton worked out that the force decreases if the objects are farther apart. He also proved that Kepler's measurements of how planets move around the sun were due to gravity.

Newton was able to explain how the moon's gravity moved water on Earth to cause ocean tides.

Mass and Weight

The theory also made clear that **mass** and **weight** are different, although non-scientists often use them to mean the same thing. Mass is the amount of material that something is made from and we usually measure it in ounces or pounds (grams or kilograms). Weight measures the force of gravity on an object. For example, if you travelled to the moon, your mass would not change. However, you would weigh much less because the moon is smaller than Earth, and its force of gravity is weaker.

Newton's theory was published in 1687 in the Philosophiae Naturalis Principia Mathematica.

REACTIONS AND RIFTS

Isaac Newton was a genius, but he could also be a very difficult man. Any other scientist who dared to criticize Newton's ideas could find himself in a fierce argument. Newton could hold grudges for a very long time.

Halley's Support

Newton's most enthusiastic supporter, Edmond Halley, was a brilliant scientist himself. He did everything he could to persuade Newton to put his ideas in a book. Halley even paid for Newton's *Principia* to be printed.

Comets have been observed in the sky for millions of years. Edmond Halley used Newton's theory to figure out that the same comet orbits the sun every 76 years. It was named Halley's Comet.

Robert Hooke and Isaac Newton were both members of the Royal Society, which started in the 1660s. The Royal Society is still made up of many leading scientists.

Hooke's Anger

Not everyone was so happy when they read Newton's theory. Robert Hooke (1635–1703) was one of Britain's leading scientists, but Hooke and Newton were also bitter rivals. Hooke accused Newton of stealing his ideas for the theory of gravity. Newton accepted that the ideas of Hooke and other scientists had helped him with his work. However, the theory was more complete than anything his rival had done.

Sir Isaac

Newton's discoveries made him a national hero. In 1693, health problems forced Newton to give up his research. He moved to London and became president of the Royal Society. In 1705, he was honored by Queen Anne and became Sir Isaac Newton.

But Why?

Sir Isaac had left plenty of work for other scientists. He had shown the effect of gravity, but he had not tried to explain what caused it. How could objects be made to move if there was only empty space between them?

In Newton's time, astronomers only knew of six planets orbiting the sun. His theory helped them to make more discoveries.

Hard to Accept

For this reason, some European scientists could not accept Newton's theory. Maybe there was an invisible fluid in space linking all the stars and planets, some argued. Others suggested that there were clouds of invisible particles, or "corpuscles," moving things around in space. At that time, they had no way of visiting or testing outer space to see if this was true.

HENRY CAVENDISH

Henry Cavendish (1731–1810) came from a rich family. This gave him the money and time to spend his life experimenting in many areas of science. In the 1790s, he used a special pendulum to try to measure the gravitational force between objects. In the late 1700s, Cavendish also carried out an experiment to "weigh the Earth." The experiment became known as the Cavendish experiment.

EINSTEIN EXPLAINS

For more than 200 years, scientists based their work on Newton's Theory of Universal Gravitation. Astronomers studying the night sky could see that the orbit of the planet Uranus around the sun was being affected by the gravitational pull of a massive object they could not see. In 1846, the planet Neptune was discovered. Neptune's gravity was changing the orbit of Uranus.

But no one had come up with a way to explain how gravity worked, until a young German-born genius in Switzerland came up with a theory that took Newton's work to the next level.

Neptune was discovered by German astronomer Johann Galle. However, France's Urbain Le Verrier and Britain's John Adams had already suspected that Neptune existed because of the effect of its gravity.

Einstein's Idea

In 1907, Albert Einstein sat at work in a **patent office** in Bern, Switzerland. The young clerk was already becoming well known for his important new theories. He was struck by the thought that a falling person feels weightless. This led him to think about gravity. Finally, it led to a theory that solved many questions that Newton had left unanswered.

ALBERT EINSTEIN

Albert Einstein (1879–1955) did not show early signs of changing the world. He found primary school difficult and left his secondary school early. He left Germany and eventually settled in Switzerland. He finally finished school before taking a job in an office. This gave Einstein time to think and come up with the theories that made him famous.

Moon

Earth

According to Einstein, Earth's gravity bends space–time (shown here as a net). The moon is caught up in Earth's gravitational force.

Einstein Explains Space and Time

Einstein published his General Theory of Relativity in 1916. His Special Theory of Relativity had already looked at how space and time worked, but it took him 10 years to create a new theory about gravity.

Space–Time

In his theory, Einstein presented the whole universe as a vast area of what he called space–time. He described how gigantic objects like the sun and planets can bend this space–time to create mountains and valleys. Earth's gravity makes a valley in space–time. This appears to drag things towards it and shapes how all objects move in space around the planet. Earth is actually traveling in a straight line, but the sun bends space so the straight line ends up going around the sun.

A Delay in Testing

When Einstein first explained his theory in 1916, it was headline news. But there was a problem. World War I had begun in 1914 and this stopped Einstein from traveling to make the measurements he needed to support his theory. He had to wait until 1919 to observe an **eclipse** of the sun and measure the effects of gravity on light.

MERCURY MYSTERY

The orbit of Mercury around the sun puzzled scientists before Einstein's new theory. Mercury is the closest planet to the sun but it didn't quite fit into Newton's calculations. Some astronomers believed there might be an unknown planet affecting Mercury's orbit. However, Einstein's General Theory solved the mystery once and for all by showing that the sun's bending of space changed Mercury's orbit very slightly.

Still Testing

Einstein's General Theory of Relativity changed people's understanding of the universe and *how* gravity holds it together. Newton had explained how planets and other objects moved. Einstein explained *why* this happened. He suggested things that could not be proved with equipment at the time, so scientists are still testing many of his ideas.

Black Holes

Scientists used Einstein's theory to develop some very strange ideas. A collapsed star could change space–time so much that nothing could escape from its gravity, not even light. All we would see is a **black hole** in space. Scientists **predicted** that black holes existed long before they actually found any.

Scientists believe that once a huge star stops burning, it can collapse in on itself due to gravity, becoming a black hole.

Making Waves

In 2016, 100 years after Einstein revealed his theory, scientists discovered that another of Einstein's ideas was correct. Using very sensitive equipment, they were able to detect a collision between two black holes in deep space. This giant crash created gravitational waves in space, as predicted by Einstein.

TIME TRAVEL

There are still mysteries to solve in the universe. Some people believe that objects with extremely strong gravity could bend space–time so much that time travel would be possible. Space–time could contain **wormholes** that are bridges to another part of time and space. At the moment, wormholes are just a hypothesis, as we don't yet have evidence that they exist.

WHY DOES GRAVITY MATTER?

Before the work of scientists like Galileo, Newton, and Einstein, people knew almost nothing about gravity, but they were still affected by it. So why is the theory so important?

Astronomy

Knowing how our universe fits together is important in itself. Astronomers can study and map the orbits of planets, comets, and **asteroids** around the sun. They can find out if any smaller objects in space are in danger of crashing into our planet.

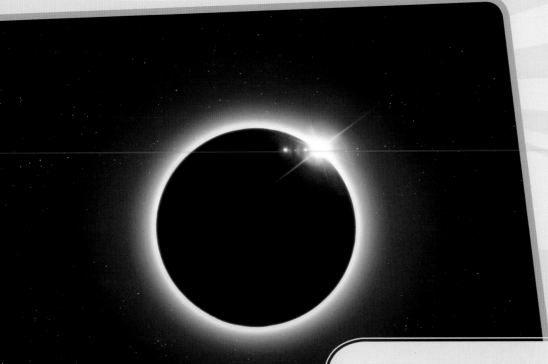

Understanding gravity means astronomers can predict eclipses, when the moon covers the sun.

Astronauts in space feel weightless because they are falling at high speed just like the spacecraft they are traveling on.

Space

Understanding gravity is important for many other areas of modern technology. If you want to launch a rocket into space, it has to move at very high speeds to avoid being pulled back to Earth by the planet's gravity. To stay in orbit around Earth, a spacecraft has to be traveling at about 17,500 miles (28,000 kilometers) per hour.

Satellites

Spacecraft are not just about putting astronauts in space. The signals for our phones and TVs are bounced off satellites orbiting our planet.

USING GRAVITY

Scientists have found some ways in which our knowledge of gravity can help us to travel to distant planets. Rather than taking the most direct route through space, some spacecraft are sent on winding voyages that seem to take them millions of miles in the wrong direction. Actually, by using the gravity of planets and stars, they can save fuel and travel faster.

QUIZ

1. What is the name for scientists who study stars and planets?

2. Which American astronaut played golf on the moon?

3. Which German scientist plotted the orbits of the planets in the solar system?

4. According to Galileo's experiments, which objects fall faster — heavier or lighter ones?

5. Why did Isaac Newton leave Cambridge University in 1665?

6. What fruit may have been important in Newton's research on gravity?

7. Who accused Isaac Newton of stealing his ideas?

8. What delayed Einstein's plans to test his General Theory of Relativity?

9. Which German scientist discovered the planet Neptune?

10. What did scientists discover in 2016 that had been predicted by Einstein?

For the answers to this quiz, see page 31

TIMELINE

1543   Nicolaus Copernicus publishes his theory that Earth and other planets orbit around the sun

1564   Birth of Galileo, who investigated the effect of gravity on falling objects and made discoveries about the shape of the solar system

1571   Birth of Johannes Kepler, whose theories about the movements of the planets led to later discoveries about gravity

1665   Isaac Newton starts work on his theory about gravity, according to legend after seeing an apple fall from a tree

1687   Newton publishes his Theory of Universal Gravitation

1790s Henry Cavendish uses a pendulum to measure gravitational force between objects

1846   Discovery of the planet Neptune after astronomers found that the planet's gravity was affecting the orbit of the planet Uranus

1916   Albert Einstein publishes his General Theory of Relativity, building on Newton's work to explain how gravity affects the Universe

1919   Einstein proves one of the main parts of his theory by measuring the effects of gravity on light during a solar eclipse

2016   Astronomers discover gravitational waves

GLOSSARY

alchemy—the attempt by early scientists to turn metals into gold

asteroid—the lumps of rock and metal that orbit the sun, which can be many miles across

astronomy—the study of the stars, planets, moons, and other objects in space. People who study stars and planets are called astronomers.

black hole—an area of space with such a strong gravitational field that not even light can escape from it

comet—a lump of ice and rock that orbits the sun

eclipse—a solar eclipse occurs when all or part of the sun is hidden from view by the moon

evidence—a collection of information or facts that prove if something is true or not

force—the push or pull on an object that results from its interaction with another object

gravity—the force that pulls objects towards each other. Big objects like planets have much stronger gravity than smaller objects.

hypothesis—a suggested scientific explanation for how or why something happens, which can then be tested

mass—the amount of matter that makes up an object

orbit—the path of a planet or star around a larger body like the sun

patent office—an office which decides upon and issues patents, for example to register new inventions

pendulum—a weight on a string or pole that swings at a steady rate. Pendulums were used to drive the mechanism of clocks.

predict—to expect a certain result

Roman Catholic Church—the Christian church that has the Pope as its head

solar system—the sun, the planets and other objects that are in orbit around it

theory—a scientific idea with evidence to back it up

vacuum—a space containing no matter, including gasses such as air

weight—the force on an object due to gravity, so weight changes if an object is in a location with more or less gravity

wormhole—a rip or hole in space which may make time travel possible

READ MORE

BOOKS

Hunter, Nick. *Is Time Travel Possible?* Top Secret. North Mankato, Minn.: Capstone Press, 2016.

Pascal, Janet. *Who Was Isaac Newton*? St. Louis, Miss.: Turtleback Books, 2014.

Rooney, Anne. *You Wouldn't Want to Live Without Gravity!* St. Louis, Miss.: Turtleback Books, 2014.

Stowell, Louie. *The Usborne Official Astronaut's Handbook*. London, England: Usborne, 2015.

Turner, Tanya. *Who Was Albert Einstein?* CreateSpace Self , 2017.

INTERNET SITES

Use Facthound to find Internet sites related to this book.

Visit *www.facthound.com*

Just type in 9781410987297 and go!

Check out projects, games and lots more at
www.capstonekids.com

ANSWERS TO QUIZ

10. Gravitational waves

1. Astronomers; **2.** Alan Shepard; **3.** Johannes Kepler; **4.** Neither – in a vacuum all objects fall at the same rate; **5.** He left because of an outbreak of plague; **6.** An apple; **7.** Robert Hooke; **8.** World War I; **9.** Johann Galle;

INDEX

Aristotle 8
astronomy 9, 26

black holes 24–25

Cavendish, Henry 19, 29
comets 13,16, 26
Copernicus, Nicolaus 9, 10, 29

Einstein, Albert 21–25, 26, 29
elements 9
experiments 7, 11, 12, 19

Galilei, Galileo 10–11, 12,
    26, 29
General Theory of Relativity
    22, 24, 29
gravitational force 7, 19, 29

Halley, Edmond 13, 16
Hooke, Robert 17

Kepler, Johannes 9, 14

moon 7, 14, 15

Newton, Isaac 5, 12–14, 16–
    19, 20, 21, 23, 24, 26

orbits 7, 8, 9, 10, 20, 23, 26,
    27, 29

pendulums 11, 19, 29

planets 4, 7, 8, 9, 14, 19, 22,
    23, 24, 26, 27, 29
    Earth 6, 7, 8–9, 10, 14, 15,
        19, 22, 27, 29
    Jupiter 10
    Mercury 23
    Neptune 20, 29
    Uranus 20, 29
predictions 24, 25

satellites 27
scientists 4, 5, 9, 14, 17, 18,
    19, 20, 23, 24, 25, 26, 27
Shepard, Alan 7
solar system 9, 29
spacecraft 27
sun 7, 8, 9, 14, 20, 22, 23, 26

telescopes 10
Theory of Universal
    Gravitation 13–14, 20, 29

BOOK CHARGING CARD

Accession No. _____ Call No. _____

Author _____

Title _____

Date Loaned	Borrower's Name	Date Returned